OPERANTICS

Fun and Games for the Opera Buff

BY WILLIAM J. BROOKE

Illustrated by Andrzej Czeczot

Design and Production
Anthony LaSala

Published by Spectacle Lane Press

CONTENTS

⟶

CONTENTS

INTRODUCTION

It has often been remarked, and with great truth, that opera is a combination of all the arts: music, drama, dance, painting, and sculpture. What is rarely mentioned is that opera represents these art forms at their very worst, in its overwrought lushness, hammy melodrama, hack choreography, and cheaply sensational stage settings.

Watching a really ripe performance is like enjoying a truly bad movie, say "Plan Nine from Outer Space." We are not for a moment taken in by it, but rather are swept up by its sheer *chutzpah* to a higher (or at least different) plane, where our ordinary critical faculties are suspended and we take a sensual pleasure in what we know makes no sense at all.

Opera is ridiculous. You have to admit that right off, or you can never learn to love it.

I once sang the role of Pang (or Pong—I could never remember) in *Turandot* in a big house. I was dressed in garish robes, with heavy Chinese makeup and a sort of green painted-on mask, mincing about, laughing maniacally, and singing at the top of my lungs in Italian for a thousand people who were really just waiting to hear "Nessun dorma" but didn't know it was still two acts away. They were having a good time and so was I. Life shouldn't all make sense.

I've seen a lot of books about opera that say how wonderful and great and artistic it is. I've written this book about how ridiculous opera is because I like it too much to go along with all that other nonsense. If you can't laugh at opera, you have no sense of humor; and if you can't enjoy opera, you have no sense of wonder.

This book is dedicated to Larry Raiken, who taught me to laugh at and to appreciate opera; and to Lynne, who gives me reason to appreciate everything else.

A SHORT, REASONABLY ACCURATE HISTORY OF OPERA

About 1580, a group of scholars and full-time amateurs met and called themselves the Florentine Camerata, apparently in hopes of starting a photography club. Frustrated by the shortage of Fotomat franchises around the Ponte Vecchio, they invented opera instead.

They intended to revive ancient Greek drama by having the actors sing the words in a tuneless sort of way, with a few instruments droning along. In contrast to the complex polyphonic musical style of the time, the music was to be subservient to the word. There were, needless to say, more poets than composers in the group. The members actually produced several operas, starting with Peri's *Dafne* in 1597. No box office receipts are extant, but it is safe to say that Peri's amateur status remained intact.

The first opera that is still sometimes performed today came along about ten years later when Monteverdi composed *La Favola d'Orfeo*. He was successful because he used a larger orchestra, more complex musical forms, and catchier tunes. So much for reviving Greek drama.

"Opera" in Italian means "work," and we see already the true derivation of the term: "If it works, use it." This has been the true artistic credo of all the great operatic composers, men who distinguished themselves by chucking theory (and often even rationality) out the window as soon as they got a tune in their heads.

In France, opera caught on quickly, with works imported from Italy or homegrown by Lully and Rameau. French royalty had long loved ballet extravaganzas, and it seemed but a short step from people leaping about instead of talking, to people shrieking instead of talking. The French were, and are, rather snobbish about their language, so they insisted that all operas must be performed in French and set with as little distortion of the language as possible. One syllable to one note was the rule, which didn't make the singing any more intelligible, of course, but it was nice to know the mother tongue wasn't being abused.

Back in Italy in the early eighteenth century, Scarlatti invented the *da capo* aria: The singer sang an A section, then a contrasting B section, and then went back and sang the whole A section again with even more ornamentation. Every number was a showstopper, in the worst possible sense. A person driven out of his head by this musical practice was said to have been "dacapotated."

Opera seria was the order of the day in aristocratic circles. This fairly rigid form told stories from the Greeks and Romans with lofty and elevated morals and emotions. Picture *Conan the Barbarian* with less blood and a castrato warbling the Arnold Schwarzenegger role and you have some idea of how dramatically involving this could be. Handel had the good sense, at least in England, to write *opera seria* in Italian so no one would know what was going on.

The form reached its height (or whatever) with the works of Metastasio. Metastasio was a poet who wrote a series of libretti considered so perfect that dozens of composers right down to Mozart set exactly the same works. He established the standard format of a little bit of plot followed by a

Dacapotated

big *da capo* aria or ensemble that let the audience in on the character's state of mind or lack thereof.

The plot part was usually composed as *secco* recitative, during which the orchestra went out on a break, except the harpsichordist, who practiced chords while the singers crammed as many words into as little tune as possible. "Secco" means "dry," which is apt, but another interpretation supports a close relationship (subjectively if not etymologically) to the term "psycho": a few minutes of *secco* puts one in a distinctly Tony Perkins frame of mind.

Fortunately, there were also more popular operatic forms. *Opera buffa* in Italy, *opéra comique* in France, and *singspiel* in Germany all grew from musical-comedy-like mixtures of dialogue and popular songs. These were to *opera seria* as *Laverne and Shirley* is to *Masterpiece Theatre*; it remained for Mozart to compose *The Mary Tyler Moore Show*.

Wolfgang Amadeus Mozart used his great powers of musical characterization to raise the *opera buffa* and *singspiel* to the level of art. As a reward, his royal patrons let him die in poverty, but his music long outlasted any of them. Today, his are the earliest operas to hold a place in the regular repertory, his music is heard everywhere, and movies are based on his middle name.

The other operatic genius of the mid-eighteenth century was Christoph Willibald Gluck, who left Austria for Paris, where he was lionized for raising the dramatic and poetic values of *opera seria*. World-renowned in his day, his work is now seldom performed. Moreover, it is impossible to imagine *Willibald* winning the Oscar for Best Picture. Such are the ups and downs of public taste.

The nineteenth century brought the age of *bel canto*, "beautiful singing," in Italy. Gioacchino Rossini ushered it in with his sparklingly melodic comedies and melodically sparkling tragedies. It is necessary to consult the program to know if the opera one is hearing is comic or tragic.

Rossini was a composer of such monumental laziness that he wrote a treatise on composing overtures that recommended borrowing one from another opera rather than composing anything new. He practiced what he preached in his masterpiece, *Il Barbiere di Siviglia (The Barber of Seville)*, in which five major numbers had appeared in other operas and the overture had been used already for not one but two previous productions.

Rossini made several technical innovations in his operas. He discarded the *da capo* aria in favor of the two-part *cavatina* (slow) plus *cabaletta* (fast). He also added more elaborate accompaniments to recitative sections. Both innovations were unpopular with the musicians' union, which valued its recitative breaks and liked *da capo* repeats, as they meant less music to learn, but his changes have endeared Rossini to the audience ever since.

At the age of 37, when he had amassed enough money and esteem, he stopped composing and seriously devoted the remaining thirty-nine years of his life to having a good time. He succeeded, leaving the recipe for Tournedos Rossini as his final legacy to mankind.

The melodic standard of Italian *bel canto* after Rossini was upheld by Donizetti and Bellini. Everyone wondered how they could write the amazingly beautiful and difficult mad scenes for which their operas were

known. Then Bellini was committed to an asylum, and everyone stopped wondering.

The French, meanwhile, continued to prefer their native product. The emphasis was on heroic subjects and spectacular scenic effects in the operas of Spontini, Halévy, and Meyerbeer. With typical modesty, the French called their operas Grand Opera.

When such authentic geniuses as Verdi and Wagner produced operas in Paris, they inserted ballets in the later acts. This practice was in keeping with the long-standing tradition of young Parisian rakes, who after dinner would drop by the opera house in time to see their girlfriends performing in the *corps de ballet*. As one of the few comprehensible and even commendable traditions in the long history of opera attendance, this one has of course fallen out of favor.

Of the later nineteenth century one need only say Verdi and Wagner. Verdi was the culmination of the Italian melodic tradition coupled with dramatic and nationalistic fervor. Wagner created a new form, "music drama," which did away with separate numbers and was a single melodious flow from beginning to end with the use of *leitmotifs*, or short themes, as the unifying factor in the orchestration.

Unfortunately, it is today acceptable to like both composers. In the good old days, an opera fan was passionately committed to one or the other and ready to have a go at anyone who felt differently. This passion was the pleasure of all serious critics and musical enthusiasts at the end of the century. Every performance was not only an opportunity to hear nice music but to hurl either epithets or punches, according to one's preference.

Verdi was a dramatic and musical genius whose great humanity flowed through all his work; Wagner was a pompous, dull, long-winded theoretician whose personal life was an affront to all good taste. Or, Wagner was a prophet of the future whose music and life could not be judged by old standards and whose mythic works tapped the collective unconscious; Verdi was a barrel-organ tunesmith.

→

Librettist's Typewriter

After Verdi in Italy came the *verismo* operas. These were thought to be more real-life dramas, offering sordid plots in every-day settings. *Cavalleria Rusticana* and *I Pagliacci* are the prime exemplars of this *National Enquirer* school of opera.

In the twentieth century, the Verdi-Wagner dichotomy was carried on by Giacomo Puccini's melodious theatricality and Richard Strauss' spectacularly orchestrated music dramas. No other twentieth-century composers have found a firm niche in the popular operatic repertory. Alban Berg is highly regarded by serious musicians, but the audience has never really responded to his brand of serial music, so-called, some have suggested, because it sounds like snap, crackle, and pop. Benjamin Britten has also written some good operas, but unfortunately they are in English, so the audience knows what is going on.

Four centuries of opera, yet a huge portion of the active repertory was composed in the less than 150 years from Mozart to Strauss, and virtually none in the first two hundred years or the last fifty. Audiences don't seem to want anything too old or too new; it's all borrowed and, plotwise, rather blue. The need for novelty is often filled by radical reworkings of old favorites like the *Flying Dutchmans* in outer space and *Rigolettos* on Wall Street.

What makes the best operas endure? Tunefulness, spectacular vocal effects, great orchestrations, and opportunity for scenic and costume display. Somewhere, certain Florentines who wanted to revive the simplicity and directness of Greek drama are turning over in their cameratas.

Even today, the true opera fanatic will choose one or the other of these positions to derive the greatest pleasure from the works. (It is perfectly all right to convert to the other side periodically, so as not to miss out on anything.) A Wagner adherent who was resolutely of the old school once sent off to the Texaco Opera Quiz the question "Why is Verdi so bad?" For some reason it was never used.

THE TEN MOST OFTEN ASKED QUESTIONS ABOUT OPERA

(And Their Answers)

Filet Mignon

1. Why are operas sung in foreign languages?

To preserve the purity of the vowel sounds and to disguise the stupidity of the lyrics.

2. Why are opera singers so fat?

Singers need large resonating spaces and great reserves of energy and, most important, they eat too much.

3. Why is everything in opera sung? Isn't that unnatural, since people don't sing in real life?

Opera is about adultery, lust, incest, infanticide, patricide, fratricide, matri-cide, uxoricide, regicide, ghosts, curses, high treason, and homicidal madness. After all that, if singing seems unnatural to you, you have odd priorities.

4. Why are operatic plots so outrageous?

It's not unreasonable to shriek your lungs out if you realize you just threw your baby in the fire; it looks silly if you're just discussing the weather.

5. Why are opera tickets so expensive?

The opera house is one of the last bastions of social order. If tickets weren't expensive, anyone who wanted to hear an opera could attend.

6. Why do people dress so uncomfortably at the opera?

To keep themselves awake.

7. Why are operas so long?

Operas were composed to provide an entire evening of entertainment, sex, and violence. This was before the invention of *Dynasty*.

8. Why is the music so loud?

To distract you from the acting.

9. Why is the acting so bad?

Artistic consistency.

10. Who really likes opera?

Insomniacs.

HOW TO SURVIVE AN OPERA

1. Don't read the libretto. It will only confuse and depress you.

2. Don't listen to the music. Either you'll like it or you won't, so why let it spoil your anticipation.

3. Run three miles the day before. Sitting through an opera requires top physical conditioning. Any circulatory difficulty can result in loss of feeling in the extremities, severe cramps, lack of oxygen to the arteries in the head, and, in extreme cases, brain death, though such an occurrence would make you indistinguishable from the rest of the audience.

4. Get plenty of sleep the night before. A ten-minute nap at a three-hour opera will set you back five bucks, and you'll probably miss the only good aria.

5. Call in sick at work and get more sleep. It is physically impossible to sweat blood all day at the office and then try to care about Lucy Lammermoor's dating problems.

6. Wear clothes that you can loosen surreptitiously. Air flow is important in surviving an opera. One of those magician's shirts that you can pull off without removing your jacket would be ideal.

7. Eat lightly, drink sparingly, and (more important than all the rules combined) go to the bathroom before the opera starts. If this last needs to be explained to you, you've never sat through an opera.

OPERA ETIQUETTE

Attending an opera is far more than merely viewing a performance. For many operagoers it has very little to do with the performance at all. It is therefore important to behave appropriately.

Your performance as an operagoer is constantly being judged by your fellows. In fact, during certain passages (such as the entire second act of *Die Walküre*), the audience will probably pay far more attention to those around them than to anything happening onstage. We therefore present some simple guidelines for opera etiquette, based on close observation of actual behavior at the opera.

1. Do not whisper during the performance. This rule cannot be emphasized strongly enough. Absolutely no whispering, unless, of course, you think of something that you might forget by intermission. Or something really funny. Or it's a dull passage that you know no one cares about anyway.

2. If someone else whispers, it is your duty to shush him as loudly as possible. The sibilants in a "Shh!" carry wonderfully and in addition will serve as a warning for everyone in the opera house who might be thinking of whispering.

3. If you feel an urge for a cellophane-wrapped candy or cough drop, there's no earthly reason why you should wait five minutes for the intermission. But be considerate of others around you: the shock of unwrapping it all at once could spoil their concentration, so take as long as possible, thereby spreading the distraction and making it more bearable. Also, be sure to fold the wrapper carefully before putting it away.

4. You've paid for your seat; make full use of it. Spread out over both arms. The person next to you will respect you for taking charge. Also remember you've purchased the air rights along with the seat, so shift position as often as possible, forward, back, and to either side. Regular shifting allows you every conceivable view of the stage and will give the people behind you good exercise.

5. Speaking of exercise, at intermissions, exit on the side that will allow the greatest number of people to stand up to let you pass. If possible, forget something at your seat so that you can go back for it. Stop and talk to your companion when you're half-way to the aisle, thus letting everyone stand longer. And return to your seat just after the lights have dimmed, when people think they've had their last chance for a good stretch. Your arrival as the music begins will offer an unexpected opportunity to get the blood flowing.

6. Intermission is also the time to improve your seating. If you have noticed that a better seat is vacant (you should devote most of the first act to this), you have a perfect right to grab it. If the ticketholder arrives for the second act, give him a hard time for having the nerve to show up this late and make you lose the chance for another seat. If someone else has taken your seat when you return to it, demand that the usher throw him out.

7. Hum along with the opera only at a passage that everybody has heard so many times they would surely prefer to hear your version.

8. Don't tap your foot, but do cross your legs and jiggle them in time to the music. If the seats are properly joined, this movement can often be felt through half the row, giving

Monster of the Opera

Birthday of a Tenor

everyone an impressive demonstration of your sense of rhythm. It is also good to make small conducting motions, and especially impressive if you conduct the music as it should be conducted instead of the way it is being performed.

9. The experienced operagoer will be able to produce a wide range of noises in the mouth, nose, and throat. Loud, rhythmic breathing is effective during exciting passages. *Carmen* offers many opportunities for castanet-like tongue-clicking. Suck air between the teeth during syncopated passages. Swish saliva around your mouth for an even subtler effect. Sniff on every other downbeat. Yawn during quiet passages. The possibilities are endless, but for maximal musical effect they should be carefully rehearsed at home, perhaps with records. Not for the novice.

10. Do not stay to the end of the curtain calls. If possible, do not stay to the end of the opera. Leave as soon as possible after the last major aria. Allow the greatest number of people to stand (see above), and mumble about making the last train. Everyone will respect your good taste for knowing there's nothing of interest left to hear. The artists certainly shouldn't mind, since if everyone left they'd get home earlier.

THE GREAT SINGERS' ACTING CORRESPONDENCE COURSE

You've spent ten years and thousands of dollars learning to sing and here it is your big operatic debut and you suddenly clap your hand to your head and exclaim, "Oh, my gosh, I've been so busy, I forgot to learn how to act!" No problem! Many great singers have found themselves in the same situation. What did they do? They dialled our toll-free number to get the course that can make anyone a great operatic actor with a few simple techniques.

These rules were scientifically determined by feeding the movements and expressions of the great singing actors into a computer. This is what it spit out:

1. Expressions:

A. Scrunch your forehead up, getting a nice furrow between your eyebrows. Good. That takes care of hatred, determination, and all forms of general intensity.

B. Open your eyes wide, let your eyebrows fly way up, and open your mouth a little. Hey, you're a natural at this! That's all you need for love and astonishment.

That wasn't so hard, was it? Now give your face a rest while we work on your hands.

2. Hands:

A. Make a fist. Relax. Do it again. Now the other hand. Now—this is tricky—both at once. Great! You've done this before, right?

B. Pretend you're shaking hands. No, don't look for someone to shake with. Remember, we're acting. Hand relaxed, fingers together, thumb at an angle. Now a tough one—do it left-handed. Yes, it is hard, but you'll get the hang of it. Try saying, "Hi, Lefty," if it helps.

C. Now an easy one—point right. No, index finger. That's it. Point left. Right. Left. Right. Left. Up. Down. Thought I'd

catch you there. Great, no sweat.

D. Splay all your fingers out straight like a starfish. Wiggle them. That's not part of the gesture, it's just for fun.

Rest those hands. Crack your knuckles if you'd like, but get those arms working.

3. Arms:

A. Straight out to the side. One. The other. Both.

B. Straight forward. One. The other. Both.

C. Bend your elbows so your hands are over your heart, one, then the other.

D. Now at your temples, left first this time, then right, then both.

E. Arms straight up. Hold it ... hold it ... let 'em drop. Which leads to...

F. Arms straight down.

Okay, shake 'em out, loosen up. What's that you're grumbling? When do you finish limbering up and get to the acting? Here's a surprise for you—you've just finished the acting course! That's right, you've done all the important stuff. Now all you have to do is put it together in the right combinations and you're an actor.

What? You don't believe it? Okay, doubting Thomas, your wife is fooling around with a soldier and you swear vengeance before heaven: 1A, 2A, 3C right; 2C, 3E left. What does it mean? Scrunch your face, clench your right hand over your heart, point your left at the sky, and, if your greasepaint is the right shade, you're doing Otello.

Now she's dead and you find out she was actually faithful all the time: expression 1B, both hands 2B, arms 3C, and you're remembering how much you loved her. If it drives you mad, expression 1A, both hands 2A, arms 3D so your fists are clenched at your temples. If her dead bell torments you, just change your hands to 2B and slip them behind your ears.

That's it, you're acting. Feels great, right? If you're getting a headache, just don't clench your forehead so much in 1A. No reason to suffer just to act, you know.

Now all you have to do is go through the score of the opera and have someone tell you what you're singing about so you can note each emotion and the corresponding actions. It's not necessary to know what each word means. Just get a general idea of what's happening.

Here's a sample from *Il Trovatore* to get you started:

TEXT	WHAT'S HAPPENING	ACTION
Di quella pira l'orrendo foco	They're getting ready to burn your mother on the hill, so you're pretty upset.	1A 2B 3A Both
tutte le fibre m'arse, avvampò!	Every fibre of your being is shook up.	2B 3C Right

Italian	Direction	Code
Empi, spegnetela, o ch'io fra poco	You're swearing vengeance.	2C 3E Left
col sangue vostro la spegnerò.	You'll put out the fire with their blood. No joke! I'm not making this up, you know.	2C 3F Left
Era già figlio prima d'amarti;	This is addressed to your girlfriend, but she's usually long gone by now, so just yearn straight out toward the audience.	1B 2B 3B Both
non può frenarmi il tuo martir!	It's not exactly clear what you're saying, but it's pretty intense.	1A
Madre infelice, corro a salvarti,	Walk (We haven't covered this, but go with your best instincts) a few steps toward the fire wherever it is: You're coming to save her!	2C 3A Right or Left as needed 2A 3C with the other
o teco almeno corro a morir!	You'll save her or die, but you have to finish the song first, so stop walking.	2A 3C Left 2C 3E Right
All'armi!	When the chorus comes in, shake hands with everybody and don't sing until the last phrase. And don't worry about your expression; the high C will take care of that.	2D 3A Both

That's basically it. The rest is icing on the cake. In the next lesson, we'll cover how to act more slowly for Wagner; how to do a dramatic lurch when cutting off high notes; how to keep your partner in a love duet from interfering with your singing and acting; and two new expressions for curtain calls only (sincerely moved and haughtily uncaring).

Remember, they came to hear you sing. If they wanted acting, they'd be home watching *Dynasty*.

GREAT ANIMAL OPERAS

Pigfried

Everyone loves to see an elephant or two in *Aida*, a lap dog in Manon's boudoir, or the occasional ass (non-singing variety) hanging around the main square in *Cavalleria*. But few of us today realize that the craze for animals in opera was so great at one time that entire operas were written for them. Janáček's *The Cunning Little Vixen* is as close as we come today, and it cheats by having the animals played by people. (The people are also played by people.)

The following operas were all written for, about, and, in some cases, by animals.

Calfalleria Ruspicatta (the only **vealismo** opera)

Fidoleo (a greasy dog story)

Die Micetersinger von Nürnberg

Pigfried

Arfeo ed Eweridice (which created a brief fad for sheepdogs in opera)

L'Anaconda (a disaster—the hero swallowed his soprano on opening night, then slept through the rest of the run)

I Pigliacci (often served with **Calfalleria**, above)

Die Zauberfloater (the only whale opera, usually performed in translation as **The Magic Fluke**)

Ernanny (Verdi kids around in a parody of Wagner's **Goateramadung**)

Tuska

Looweasel Miller

La Chinchilla del West

L'Amore dei Fay Wray ("The planes never got him; it was *tessitura* killed the beast")

El Amor Cujo

Fido and Aeneas

Porgy and Bass

La Wally ed Il Castor (the only known opera to be turned into a TV show, it was anthropomorphized as "Leave It to Beaver")

Porgy and Bass

KNOWING WHEN
AND HOW TO
SHOUT "BRAVO!"

Nothing better establishes your credentials as a true opera enthusiast than the skillful use of the "bravo." Although the uninitiated believe that the exclamation expresses uncontainable rapture at a singer's artistry, nothing could be further from the truth. The only reason for shouting "Bravo!" is to draw attention to yourself.

Realizing this, it is then obvious that timing is all-important. If everyone around you is bravoing, you cannot achieve your aim by joining in the chorus. At such times, it is wise to fold your arms and look around with lofty disdain.

The ideal moment for a bravo is in the second's hush after the quiet end of an aria.

This both highlights your bravo and lets the audience know that you are familiar enough with the music to know precisely when it finishes. A perfect example is Mimi's aria in the first act of *La Bohème*, which sort of trails off into recitative, and no one has ever been able to figure out when it actually finishes. Pick a spot, yell "Bravo!" and the soprano will shut up.

The one unforgivable sin in bravoing is not to know the proper gender and number ending. If you yell "Bravo!" for a woman, you are giving yourself away as a hopeless novice, since that is the masculine form. Here is a quick reference guide to avoid embarrassment.

BRAVO — Masculine, singular. May be applied to any male singer or conductor.

BRAVA — Feminine, singular. May be applied to any female singer or conductor.

BRAVI — Masculine and feminine plural. May be used to compliment everyone currently bowing. *Bravi tutti* means the same thing and is especially impressive if you can pronounce all three t's.

BRAVU — Undetermined, singular. Originally used only for castrati, this expression has long lain fallow. The recent interest in sex-change operations raises new possibilities for using this particularly obscure form.

BRAVE — Nearly plural. Cheers to everyone except the singer on the extreme left or the one in navy blue. Rarely heard outside Italy.

BRAVURA — Feminine, large. Congratulations on the singing, but lose a hundred pounds before playing another consumptive.

BRAVADO — Feminine, personal. Translates roughly as "Well done, dear." Meant to imply some intimacy, even hanky-panky, between shouter and singer. The extreme form, BRAVADOCIO, should be used only by those without fear of fisticuffs, duels, or paternity suits.

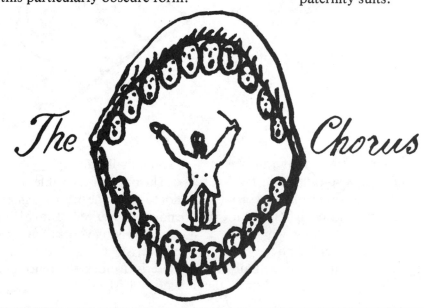

The Chorus

28

Jumpy Tosca

RIDEMANWEEP
KING OF ABYSSINIA
An Undiscovered Opera of Mozart

Ridemanweep has been away for ten years at the Trojan War. He roams around the Mediterranean for another ten years, planning to write a travel book and make a mint. Unfortunately, Homer gets exclusive rights from Odysseus and rushes a quickie ripoff into print. Disillusioned, Ridemanweep sets sail with the remnants of his crew for their native land. The winds mysteriously die and they are becalmed. An oracle informs them that, to appease the gods, they must sacrifice that which is black and white and read all over. Unable to figure out the riddle, the sailors chuck Ridemanweep over the side.

ACT I. The opera opens as Ridemanweep is washed up on a barren shoreline. He reveals all the above exposition in an exceptionally long and tedious recitative. When he comes across an old man renting beach umbrellas, he recognizes him as his former retainer, Sempridelio. Realizing he has reached home, Ridemanweep sings an aria of florid rejoicing, "Abyssinie, in tutti vecchii" ("Abyssinia, in all the old familiar places").

Once the old man can get a word in, he reveals that a great funeral is being prepared for Ridemanweep, who is believed dead. There will be much rejoicing to know that he is alive, especially by his 18-year-old son, Idiote. Ridemanweep thinks there is something odd about having an 18-year-old son when he has been away for 20 years, but mathematics has not yet been invented, so he lets it pass.

Ridemanweep decides he won't reveal himself until he knows who is faithful to him and the second act is almost over. Ridemanweep tells Sempridelio to give him clothes as a disguise. Sempridelio says he has only one set of clothes. Ridemanweep says that's all he needs and drags Sempridelio off to get them.

Idiote enters, alone. This is a trouser role; that is, a mezzo-soprano plays the role of the young man. He reveals his fear that the rival suitors for his mother's hand will consider his rightful claim to the throne as a

threat to them and that they will try to kill him. He wistfully sings the old gypsy song "Si mama mariata" ("If Mama were married").

He meets a young female cowherd named Pecunia, who pities his plight and compares it to the problems of raising cattle in "Quando mange vo" ("Whenever you eat veal"). Idiote doesn't see the connection, but has the sudden idea that if he disguises himself as a woman, he will be safe from the pretenders to the throne. He asks to borrow one of her dresses. She is disappointed but understanding, "Che faccio uomo" ("Clothes make the man"). He slips on her gown and they sing a happy duet. A chorus of Turkish pirates enters and carries them off.

Ridemanweep's wife, Uxoria, enters. She sings that she was as faithful to him as she could be, "Semper fidelis" ("Always true to you, darling, in my fashion"). The Chorus of Suitors enters, bearing gifts of fine linen, spices, and Whitman's Samplers. Depressed that Ridemanweep is dead and someone has picked out all the nuts, Uxoria can hardly bring herself to eat the rest of the chocolates. The Suitors display their various coats of arms and press their suits in the famous Ironing Chorus. Uxoria responds with the spirited aria "Un arma è come un altro" ("One coat of arms is like another").

Unnoticed by anyone but the audience, Ridemanweep joins the Suitors, who revile him for his poor clothes and funny accent. He tries to respond with calming words, "Tua madre è prostituta" ("Come, let's be friends"), but they will have none of it and draw their swords to fight with him when Uxoria stops them. Sick of all the bickering, she announces that before the funeral tomorrow she will ask three riddles and whoever answers them may wed her. All sing a chorus of rejoicing that they have finally reached the end of the act.

ACT II. The next day, Idiote and Pecunia arrive back in town. They had disguised themselves as sailors so the pirates wouldn't attempt to take liberties with them, then escaped by disguising themselves as ladies of the harem and slipping away through the seraglio. Shocked to learn that his mother has decided to choose Ridemanweep's successor that very afternoon, Idiote resolves to try to hinder her plan. After great thought, he hits on the idea of disguising himself as a suitor. Pecunia goes home to take a hot bath and try to sort it out.

Ridemanweep enters, wondering what he will do if the riddles are too obscure for him to answer, "Gli enigmi son'outre," but he figures his chances are at least equal to those of the other suitors. The Chorus of Suitors returns, boning up on books of riddles that they have checked out of the library. Having spent his youth learning to fight, Ridemanweep is unable to read and cries out despairingly, "Books, books, always books!" ("Sempre libri!").

Uxoria appears at the head of a grand staircase and everyone bows to the floor to hide their books. Uxoria explains the rules, "In questa reggia" ("In the question I read'ya"), and asks the first riddle: "What has four wheels and flies?" Everyone answers, "Two garbage chariots" ("Due carretti garbagii," often mistranslated as "two-car garage," which makes the plot even more obscure than it already is).

A chorus of general rejoicing is interrupted by the second riddle: "What has a big, black mustache, smokes a big, black cigar, and is a big pain in the neck?" Everyone passes, so she collects $50 and asks the last riddle: "What's black and white and read all over?" Ridemanweep still doesn't know this one, but everyone else shouts, "A newsparchment!" and breaks into wild rejoicing.

It appears that Uxoria will have to marry everyone except Ridemanweep, so he draws his sword and threatens to slaughter the whole company. The Suitors draw their own swords and prepare to do battle, when Neptune rises out of the sea wearing a tragic mask and warning that only the man who is a woman can stand against the stranger. As he sinks back into the sea, the Suitors sing in wonderment "Chi è quell'uomo in maschera?" ("Who is that masked man?").

Hoping to save his mother and figuring that the cryptic message must refer to him, Idiote steps forward to fight. On Ridemanweep's first thrust, Idiote's robe falls away, revealing his harem costume. The Suitors draw around with interest, but Idiote throws off his harem costume to reveal his sailor outfit. "Ecce homo," the Suitors sing as they draw back in disgust. Now quite caught up in the drama, Idiote removes his sailor costume and then the dress that Pecunia has lent him. (The orchestration at this point provides the first and perhaps only operatic use of rimshots to accompany Idiote's increasingly enthusiastic disrobing.)

Pecunia arrives just in time to prevent him from removing his Idiote costume and revealing himself as a mezzo-soprano. She explains the story of their adventures to everyone at great length, "Un balena di racconto" ("A whale of a tale"). Ridemanweep, who has been fuming at the intrusion of this subplot into his big scene, again threatens general destruction, but Uxoria steps forward and announces that there was only one man she ever knew who didn't know what was black and white and read all over. "Ridemanweep!" she cries, throwing herself into his arms. "What's red all over?" he replies.

The ladies of the Turkish harem now arrive, having followed Idiote and Pecunia in their escape. The Suitors promptly pair up with them, Idiote embraces Pecunia, and Sempridelio is given one of Idiote's costumes so he can appear in the finale. When he appears he announces that the Turkish pirates have been destroyed by a storm at sea. Ridemanweep asks if anyone can think of any plot lines unresolved. When no one can, he leads the company in the finale, "Tutto nel mondo è burla" ("All the world is burlap"). This is apparently an obscure reference to the curtain, which now falls.

Ironing Chorus

AMUSING OPERAS

L'Aughrican

Clarabella

Stereo Hi Fidelio

La Jokeonda

Giggletto

Simon Boffonegra
(renowned for its
black humor)

Daffny

**Les Monologues des
Carmelites** (early
example of
standup humor)

**The Turn of the
Screwball** (only
opera directed by
Preston Sturges)

Wozzeck

La Jokeonda

MAKING THE MOST OF INTERMISSIONS

1. The first rule of intermissions is: Run! To the bar, if you are a man; if a woman, to the bathroom. At the bathroom you will find sixty-two little old ladies in line ahead of you. At the bar, you will find what seem to be the same sixty-two little old ladies clamoring for restoratives. No one has ever determined how these senior citizens who move so slowly when blocking doorways can move so fast when the opera breaks.

2. Once you have your overpriced drink or have accepted that you aren't going to make it to the bathroom this intermission, you must find a good place to stand. Position is important, and style is everything: Get downstairs with the rich folks. Muscle up to a railing looking over the grand staircase. You want to be seen without being obvious.

3. Take a sip, breathe deeply, and make a pronouncement, it matters not what. (See "After the Opera" if you need prompting.)

You don't direct it toward anyone in particular; you're being oracular here, not conversational. You will be immediately disputed by whoever is nearby. This is good. By speaking first, you have established your credentials. You need only smirk and chuckle at what anyone else says.

4. Deposit your glass in a picturesque spot. There are two schools of thought here. One holds for perching the glass on the railing or the ashtray or the statue pedestal with the napkin folded in origami shapes; the other values the subtler touch of the glass concealed behind something so that it will escape cleaning staff notice for several weeks. Toss in a cigarette butt to truly disgust the sharp-eyed operagoer.

5. Time your departure with precision. Listen for the bells, discreetly consult your watch, and make your move at the last possible moment.

6. Fire off a final crushing rejoinder. "But then you never saw Callas, did you?" always works well, no matter what you've been discussing. Stroll off casually, then burn rubber. You don't want your exit line ruined when whoever you've been talking to has to get upstairs, too.

7. Remember to bring an umbrella or something else with a good point on it. When you're trying to get back to your seat, there will be sixty-two little old ladies moving slowly in front of you.

THE CLAQUE

The claque has existed in its non-professional form for as long as mankind has been performing. When Mog acted out his hunt of the ferocious groundhog for his bored fellow cavedwellers, it was his mother, Moa, who got things lively by hooting, beating the ground with sticks, and flinging liberal dollops of cave bear spoor at other audience members.

The Neanderthal brain couldn't recall much of Mog's recitation, but it couldn't forget the hot time in the cave that night, so Mog became known as a mighty hunter. Just so, down through history, many audiences have been fooled into believing they have witnessed something more than a workaday performance by the enthusiasm of an individual or a small group.

"Claque" is a French word meaning "applause," like the similarly onomatopoeic

English "clap." The French word is even more appropriate, however, since it also carries the sound of coins clicking together.

The First Professional Claque

The claque was accidentally invented by the Italian prima donna Juverri Grisi in 1671. When playing the lead in Lully's *Danae* at the Académie de Musique, she refused to sing anything but Italian. The French audience found this insulting and declined to applaud. Piqued, Grisi threw at the audience the first thing that came to hand. As she had just been visited by Zeus in the form of a shower of gold, it happened to be a handful of coins. The groundlings quickly found that their opinion had been hasty and applauded her wildly as she kept flinging them gold.

The next day they were back with murder in their hearts and boos on their lips after discovering that the gold coins were merely stage props, but a hasty distribution of francs ensured the success of the remainder of her run.

When the next prima donna came to town, she was greeted by a host of outstretched palms. Outraged at first, she soon realized she could get full value for her money by paying the audience not only to applaud her but also to boo the tenor. Thus was the creation of the claque completed. Within a few years, the tradition spread to all parts of the operatic world, but it was in Italy that the claque would achieve its fullest flowering.

The Tradition of Throwing Food

Throwing food was originally intended as a compliment. In 1811, claque member Luigi Paisano was deeply moved by Garcia y Vega's interpretation of *V. Lombardi alla Super Bollo*, which he had also, fortunately, been well paid to applaud. When others threw roses onto the stage, Paisano threw the only thing he had handy, a mozzarella-and-tomato sandwich his wife had packed for an intermission snack. Through blind misfortune, the tenor stepped directly into the path of the tasty but messy missile and was splattered with red and white gobs. The audience was horrified but quickly realized that a new weapon was born.

Any singer who wasn't worth his salt or who hadn't greased the right palms was fair game, as food flights became the order of the day. Sandwiches only were used at first, with ingredients varied for maximum range and splatter. They were soon followed by pies, entire cheeses, and increasingly elaborate pasta dishes, and, finally, various roast fowl and small animals, climaxing at the premier of *Il Figlio Prodigale* with the flinging by catapult of a fatted calf. The singers of the time were intimidated but well fed.

Finally, someone realized that vegetables such as the tomato and turnip were cheap, perfect for hurling, and healthier for the performers. From then on, vegetables ruled. In 1832, the fishpeddlers' union of Genoa made a determined effort to establish seafood as the missile of choice. Though it was generally agreed that fish made a satisfying splat and squid looked especially nice slithering down the proscenium, at long performances in the summertime the stench arising from the fish-filled pockets of the claque was impossible to endure. The lowly vegetable was vindicated.

The Claque Today

The claque today has fallen upon hard times. As a well-organized, rigorously disciplined group, proud of its vocal technique and pitching arms, it scarcely exists in this country. The rise of restrictive managements, oppressive propriety of the audience, and the ever-present disruptive influence of the amateur claqueur have taken their toll. The rise of television seemed briefly to offer the prospect of a golden age for the claque, but that bright hope was crushed by the invention of the laugh track.

Most claques today are more of a disorganized rabble bought with a handful of the cheapest tickets, who applaud and cheer without finesse or artistry. Only in a few small Italian provincial houses does the claque still excel, passing down its tradition from father to son. There the true opera connoisseur attends performances to hear the audience, not the singers. Only there is a performance still an adventure, and the artist who dares the claque's wrath takes his life and his lunch into his own hands.

King Burger V

MOST LUDICROUS PLOTS IN ONE SENTENCE

Refreshing Music

- Wozzeck eats peas and kills his mistress.

- Nothing happens and Mélisande dies.

- Manrico loves Leonora, who is the ward of di Luna, who hates Manrico, but because Azucena threw the wrong baby in the fire, they are actually brothers, and di Luna kills him while Leonora poisons herself and Azucena dies of satisfaction.

- Someone steals the Rhine Maidens' gold, but they get it back fifteen hours later.

- Two men disguise themselves as Albanians to see if their girlfriends will remain true to them; they won't.

- Monk meets girl, monk loses girl, monk gets nun.

- Werther mopes for three acts, then kills himself.

43

TELEPHONE OPERAS

Today, the telephone is so taken for granted it is hard to remember just what an impact it had when it was first invented. Its influence was felt even in the field of opera, most memorably in *The Telephone* and *La Voix Humaine*. But there were other, less successful operas that tried to cash in on the popularity of the invention, including:

Otellophone

Amahl and the After-Six and on Weekends Visitors (Menotti's cut-rate sequel to **The Telephone**)

Lakmé (famous for its "Alexander Graham Bell Song")

Der Ring des Telephonen: Das Ringold, Die Wallphone, Ringfried, and **Götterdämmering**

Les Dialtones des Carmelites

Touch-Tonehäuser

La Fonecalla dial West

AT&Tila, the Hun

Cosi Fone Tutti

The Extension from the Seraglio

Areacodne auf Naxos

AT&Tila

OPERATIC ROLES EVEN YOU CAN PERFORM

Okay, so you've always wanted to be in an opera, but the idea of being a spearcarrier doesn't appeal to you. Here is a list of authentic operatic roles that anyone (with a bit of cunning) can perform.

Florestan in *Fidelio* and Turandot in *Turandot*: What's that you say? These are tough roles? Well, you know what they say, "When the going gets tough, the tough get going." So don't hang around. The critical part of doing these roles is not being there for the second act. Since you don't sing in the first act, you've got it made. Develop a virus during intermission and let your cover step in. Even some of the world's greatest singers would swear by this method.

Wotan in *Götterdämmerung*: There's good and bad news about this one: good is that you don't sing a note in the whole opera but make a spectacular appearance in a sort of vision during the Immolation Scene; bad is that most cheapo modern productions cut the vision along with the horse and most of the fire.

The Prince of Persia in *Turandot*: This is a no-lose situation. You get to walk slowly across the stage while the whole chorus sings about how good-looking you are. Then, once you're offstage, you have to sing only one word, "Turandot," and since you're offstage it doesn't make any difference how awful you have to look to get the note out. If you don't have the note, it's a cinch that you'll always find some old chorus tenor who will do anything to show off his high A.

Andromache in *Les Troyens*: You get center stage for five minutes and don't have to sing a note, just pantomime about how bad you feel about the war and everything. The only drawback is having to share the stage with the kid playing your son. But after five minutes alone out there, you may find some distraction is all to the good. Bring along a puppy, too, if you feel really nervous about it.

→

The Captain in *Manon Lescaut*: Here's the ideal role. You stand there and look important while all the prostitutes board your ship. Then the tenor comes over and kneels at your feet and you get to look at him disdainfully and the whole act builds and builds. You provide the climax by singing a couple of short phrases that they usually give to some eighty-year-old baritone anyway, and then pretty music plays while you strut offstage. Forget the others; go for this one if you can.

OPERA FOR

OVERWEIGHT PERFORMERS

Ieata

Madama Butterfat

Filet Mignon

Salami

Mefistuffeta

Boris Gotenough

Increasia Borgia

La Gigonda

Cosy Fat Tushy

The Medium-Large
(by Menotti; the
role can be let out
if necessary)

Enorma

Les Hugenots

Manon L'Escargot

Don Carloads

La Sonmangiula

**The Ballad of
Baby Donut**

Das Lebersverbot
(The Ban on Liver,
an early dieting
opera by Wagner)

**Les Dialogues des
Caramelites**

Esclarmounde

La Fodderita

**Die Zaftigen Weiber
von Windsor**

**The Mother of Us
All**

La Roundine

Tonhowser

La Vache Humaine

**La Donna del
Largeo**

The Dairy Queen

Fidelicatesseno
(later shortened for
rhythmic reasons)

Mathis der Mauler
(Hindemith's opera
about an over-the-
hill wrestler)

Oreo ed Euridice

Suor Anjellyca

Thaïghs

GIUSEPPE O'REILLY
Composer and Simpleton

Giuseppe O'Reilly found his heritage both a blessing and a curse. Born in 1823 to an Irish mother and an Italian father, he was blessed with the natural lyricism of those two races, composing 62 operas before he was twenty. This constituted his Early Period. Unfortunately, his mother let him speak only Gaelic and so none of these works ever achieved widespread popularity.

At 21, in an attempt to win a broader audience, he composed *Dingo, King of Fiji*, the first opera in Esperanto. If he had waited only 43 years until Esperanto had been invented, his opera might have enjoyed a greater immediate success. However, a great stroke of luck befell him.

An itinerant German troupe of opera singers and spies lost the orchestral parts to

La Clemenza di Tito. Needing an immediate replacement on arrival in Verona, they stumbled on the original score of *Dingo* at the auction of a cheese merchant's goods, where it was being used to separate slices of cheddar. They hastily mounted the opera to great success. The Germans thought they were singing Italian; the Veronese thought it German.

No one understood it (one of the prime requirements of any serious opera), and it was a smash hit. The delighted audience dragged O'Reilly into the street, loosed the horses of his carriage, and made him pull them through the city while they sang bawdy songs.

Suddenly, productions of O'Reilly's works sprang up all over Italy, all performed in Gaelic, which everyone thought an obscure southern dialect related to Sicilian. These were all pirate productions, so O'Reilly made nothing from them. He continued to live in near poverty until the publisher Recordare offered him 50 lire per annum and all the potatoes he could eat for the rights to all his works. He gleefully accepted, bought some olive oil, and thus produced his Lyric Period.

Flush with cash and *pommes de terre*, O'Reilly devoted himself to achieving perfection in the opera of his Middle Period. He composed a single work, *Beatrice di Gioca, Queen of Middlesex and the Little Bit of Northumberland Right at the Very Top*, and responded to all commissions with a revision of the same work. Some of these were titled *Leonora di Gioca, Violetta di Gioca, Beatrice D. Gioca, Enrico di Cavatini, Arribaldo*, and *Wozzeck*.

For the Paris Opera he inserted ballet into the fourth act, which did not bother him, since the opera had only three acts. For Venice, he made the lead a castrato. For Rome, he added political overtones so the censor could cut them. For Covent Garden, he prepared a version in English, then had it translated into German so the English would not have to hear their own language sung.

The opera was a huge success everywhere it was played, and Recordare paid O'Reilly a bonus of 100 lire. He could probably have gone on composing this one opera for the rest of his life if the discovery of patriotism had not precipitated his Later than Middle but Not Quite Final Period.

O'Reilly was secretly approached by members of the Paisan Go Bragh Society. This obscure political sect held that they had discovered, through little-known theories of continental drift, that Ireland and Italy had once been united but had been severed by corrupt feudal lords and geotectonic forces. They convinced O'Reilly to fall in with their cause, and he began producing works with thinly veiled political overtones. These included *Heather of Tuscany, Giovanna di Blarney,* and *La Forza del Geologi*.

Rabid patriots scrawled the name O'Reilly on walls as an acronym for "Once Reunited Eire and Italy will Last a Lot of Years." The party actually succeeded in gaining power in one small area of Ireland, where they hired fishing boats and attempted to drag the island through the Straits of Gibraltar. However, terrible internal rifts developed over how they were going to brake once they reached the vicinity of Sardinia so they wouldn't smash into Sicily. The party disintegrated into splinter factions before it could claim more than a few centimeters of progress.

Seriously disillusioned, O'Reilly withdrew from human society. He lived quietly at Villa O'Reilly, where he devoted himself to raising a crop of shamrocks and killing snakes. For many years nothing was heard from him, but a younger generation of composers regarded him as their shining example, and he was continually pestered to return to composing.

At last he relented and produced his Final Period, an astounding series of operas composed at the age of 92. Unfortunately, he insisted on notating his own scores and, as he was completely blind by this time, the results were somewhat spotty. Some notes made it to the manuscript page, but many went onto the table, the lap dog, his own clothing and that of any visitors, the bedspread, the napkins, the piano, the walls, and, upon one occasion, the naked chest of an aspiring young soprano who attempted to offer herself at the altar of her art.

As a result, no more than three or four notes in a row could ever be performed, but all agreed on the sheer genius of those few notes. A booming trade in illicit souvenirs arose, since almost any object that could be purloined from the Villa contained a few scribbles of precious inspiration.

All of this meant little to O'Reilly, who died in poverty at the age of 98 when the shamrock crop failed. He was buried in a pauper's grave, but the pauper objected, and his body was moved to an unknown location.

Today almost none of O'Reilly's operas holds a place on the operatic stage. The judgment of history or a passing phase?

With the revival of so many lesser works by obscure composers, it can be only a matter of time before the operatic world turns its attention to Giuseppe O'Reilly, the composer who gave new meaning to the words "lesser" and "obscure."

OPERATIC RIDDLES

- **Why is Rigoletto so worried about what might happen to Gilda?**

  Because he has a bad hunch.

- **Who is the most egotistical tenor in all opera?**

  Rodolfo in *La Bohème*, who goes around singing "Me! Me!"

- **Name a famous operatic pair of ducks (not counting the "Pair-o'-dux" trio from *Pirates of Penzance*).**

  Huey and Dewey Foscari. It would have been a trio, but Louey always quacked on the high notes.

- **Why did Luisa Miller sleep late?**

  She'd heard the early bird got the Würm.

- **Why did Andrea Chénier speak out against his country?**

  Because the French people were revolting.

- **What operatic tenor always brings down the house?**

  Samson.

- **What operatic soprano refuses the baritone at first but eventually gets into the habit?**

→

Thaïs. She starts off a 10 and ends up a nun.

- **What role is too jumpy for nervous sopranos?**

Tosca.

- **Which Wagnerian opera reminds us of Stephen Foster?**

Lohengrin, because it starts and ends way down upon a swan-y river.

- **What's the difference between *Aida* and a music critic?**

One has a Nile setting; the other has seating on an aisle.

GREAT PROMOTIONAL OPERAS

We all know that most composers never achieved the wealth they deserved, many, like Mozart, dying in poverty, others, such as Wagner, always a step ahead of the bill collector. Even today's serious composers sometimes find themselves turning out advertising music to make ends meet. Few realize they are following in a noble tradition of composers' pushing products to earn a livelihood.

The following operas were all created with an eye to lucrative advertising con-

tracts. These pot-and-pan-boilers allowed their composers to pursue the true art of opera in their other, better-remembered works. This form of opera flourished from the late 1800s until the invention of the jingle in 1922 sounded its death knell and ended the tradition.

Le No-Doz di Figaro: Mozart's ever-popular tale of a valet's wedding night was followed by an unsuccessful sequel about a gardener's wedding night, **Le Nozze di Vigoro**.

La Clemenza di Frito: Mozart's only opera cereal.

Wigoletto: Verdi's outspokenly anti-royalist opera set in a beauty parlor was heavily censored and performed only in the watered-down version called **Un Ballo in Mascara**.

Hansel und Geritol: Humperdinck's charming tale of youth and age is traditionally associated with National Secretary's Week.

Ex-Laksme: Even the French found Delibes' tale of a stuck-up Hindu princess hard to swallow, although the extravagant coloratura of the famous ''Bowl Song'' always brought a flush of excitement.

Canon Lescaut: Japanese tourists with cameras visit the United States. Puccini did it much better the next year with **Land-o-Lakes Butterfly**, which he retitled **Madama** at the last moment when his sponsor pulled out.

Dristan und Isolde: Wagnerian love aroused by magic nasal sprays. Not very penetrating.

Ariadne auf Nachos: Strauss' quintessential tale of old Tijuana, highlighted by the presentation of the silver taco.

Love for Three Oranges, N.J.: Prokofiev's was the only opera commissioned by a Chamber of Commerce.

L'Incoronazione di Popiel's Pocket Fisherman: One of the earliest of commercial operas, Monteverdi's masterpiece is never performed today, calling as it does not only for a cast that can sing, but singers who can cast.

Das Rheingold: Almost the only commercial opera still in the standard repertory today and perhaps the greatest of all the beer operas, although others would accord that position to Verdi's **Falstaff**.

FAMOUS ARIAS
AND WHAT THEY
REALLY MEAN

Even if you know Italian or German, you can't possibly understand what singers are singing. Here is a quick checklist of what the big arias and ensembles are really about:

"Casta diva" from *Norma*: Unabashed self-promotion. The soprano sings that if you want someone to sing this aria, you've got to cast a diva.

"Non mi dir" from *Don Giovanni*: Don Ottavio asks if she wouldn't like to get married and Donna Anna replies, "Not me, dear!"

"Dove sono" from *Le Nozze di Figaro*: The Countess wonders how the Count could find anyone else half as attractive, since "I sound like a dove!" Earlier, she traditionally sings "Porgi amor," which is actually an interpolation in Italian of the Gershwin aria "I Loves Ya, Porgy." No one knows quite why this is interpolated, but since it's in Italian, no one cares.

"Caro nome" from *Rigoletto*: Shut up alone in her hot Italian villa, Gilda dreams of a new life in a dear little city in Alaska. Rigoletto has his own favorite city: "Pari siamo," he sings, "I love Paris." "Paris when it drizzles," the Duke chimes in, "Parmi veder le lagrime." (Ever-popular, Paris also appears in *Martha*'s famous "M'appari.") In spite of his fondness for Paris, the Duke also recalls a lovely lady he once knew in Alabama, "La donna è mobile."

"Winterstürme" from *Die Walküre*: "Winter stirs me," Siegmund sings irrelevantly, pulling a sword out of a tree and swinging it wildly. Startled, Sieglinde's contacts pop out. Siegmund drops to his knees to search, but there is a sickening crunch and Sieglinde moans accusingly, "Du bist der Lenz."

"Liebestod" from *Tristan und Isolde*: Transplanted from an earlier opera based on the Frog Prince, this music addresses the beloved amphibian.

"Che gelida manina" from *La Bohème*: The starving Bohemians can think of little but food. Here Rodolfo dreams of the jello he'll eat tomorrow. Mimi shares some of her own favorite recipes, and they finish the act by envisioning the perfect chilled wine to go with it all, "O soave fanciulla."

"O don fatale, o don crudel" from *Don Carlo*: Horrified by Carlo's admission that

Carmen

he may have given her a social disease ("Io la vidi"), Eboli squeals on Carlo's plan for taking over the numbers racket in Flanders to two rival Godfathers.

"Le veau d'or" from *Faust*: The earliest example of scat singing, Mephistopheles' aria translates literally as "Vo de o do."

"Nothung! Nothung! Neidliches Schwert!" from *Siegfried*: The heroic young tenor is infuriated at not getting any good melodies to sing: "No tune! No tune! An' I'd like to swear!"

"Mein lieber Schwan" from *Lohengrin*: Another self-promotion aria. The tenor says you'll find a full list of his recordings in his favorite book, the Schwann catalogue.

"O namenlose Freude" from *Fidelio*: Leonora and Florestan sing their unspeakable gratitude to the Viennese doctor who has cured her compulsion for wearing men's clothes.

"Près des remparts de Séville" from *Carmen*: Carmen tells Don José's fortune with cards. Aries is causing trouble in the house of Pisces, José's astrological sign. "Pray the ram parts from your house." This is also known as the *Seguidilla*, the "following" or "new deal" aria. (The only other major astrological aria is in *La Traviata*, when Violetta bemoans the problems she always has with men born in October, "Sempre libera.")

"Stride la vampa!" from *Il Trovatore*:

Azucena wistfully recalls her youth, when she was widely known for her sexy walk.

"Com'è gentil" from **Don Pasquale**: Disappointed in love, Ernesto practices his audition piece for the local oratorio society's performance of Handel's **Messiah**. He will be crushed again to learn it is the bass who sings "And the gentiles shall come to the light."

"O patria mia" from **Aida**: Aida remembers fondly the pastries she used to bake for the O'Haras on their lovely plantation, to which she will later sing her final farewell, "O terra, addio."

"Un'aura amoroso" from **Così Fan Tutte**: Ferrando longs to whisper sweet nothings into his girlfriend's loving ear.

"Donna non vidi mai" from **Manon Lescaut**: Penniless and unable to pay his rent, Des Grieux asks only one thing: that they will not give away his TV set.

"Morgendlich leuchtend" from **Die Meistersinger von Nürnberg**: The finished Prize Song in the third act is actually the German version of "Oh, What a Beautiful Morning." Earlier, when the song is still taking shape, Walther sings the second verse, "All the cattle are standing like statues," in the German "Am stillen Herd."

"Un bel di" from **Madama Butterfly**: Cio-Cio-San wistfully recalls the lovely high note she sang in her first-act entrance.

Aria of Cavaradossi

A Selection of Exhibits from

HEINRICH OSTERMAN'S
WONDERFUL
WORLD OF OPERATIC
ODDITIES
AND
MONKEY JUNGLE

→

Opera buffs love disasters. The greatest repository of mementos from the greatest operatic disasters is located not in New York or Milan but just off Route I-95 in Ocala, Florida, between McDonald's and the C-U-Later Alligator Ranch. An unlikely, whitewashed building houses the personal aggregation of Heinrich Osterman, a renowned standee and petty thief in all the great opera houses of Europe, now retired.

Though the dusty collection gives no hint of its lofty origins, what looks like a run-down flea market to the uninitiated is Mecca to the true opera lover. Here are some of the prizes of the collection and their stories.

A Bit of Burned Cloth

The smoking chorus from *Carmen* was popular, but produced no imitators. It remained for Wolf-Ferrari's *Il Segreto di Susanna*, with its plot about a girl whose secret passion is for smoking, to initiate a brief craze for smoking operas. As each new opera tried to outdo the last, such works as *Le Cig, L'Italiana con Cigari*, and *Antonio y Cleopatra* featured more smoking and stronger blends.

The craze reached an abrupt climax with the celebrated smoking chorus from *The Sicilian Vapors*, in which Madame Astorita Benedetta and sixty Sicilian peasants smoked stogies while setting dynamite charges around their village. An overly zealous stage director provided an unwanted touch of realism, thus leaving us with only a fragment of costume and smoky memories of La Benedetta.

A Small Pebble-like Object

The title character of Van Rosay's ill-fated *I Galstoni* was hurled with deadly accuracy at the composer-conductor by tenor Vittorio Ombra when he was denied an encore. *Il Giornale della Spettacolo* referred to it as Ombra's only real hit ("Ombra mighty few").

A Glass Eye

The great Ukrainian tenor Yuri Neritract lost this relic of the glassmaker's art (necessitated by a war injury) on the fateful opening night of the 1926 Moscow season. Attempting a full-voiced high E-flat in the last-act farewell of *Eugene Yetagain*, he shocked the audience and himself by bouncing his ocular accoutrement into the orchestra pit. After a moment of stunned silence, conductor Serge Syut quipped, "I know I told you to keep an eye out for me, but this is ridiculous."

A Rabbit's Foot

The weapon used to stab Scarpia in the famous Backward Tosca. Addlepata Malabrain was notoriously superstitious. When a black cat crossed her path on her way to the stage of La Fenice, she refused to go on until the managing director, Rudy Cazuti, convinced her that if she walked backward to the stage the cat could not be said to have crossed her path.

His pleasure at the ingenuity of his solution turned to astonishment when she made her first entrance onto the stage walking backward, clutching a rabbit's foot in one hand and a horseshoe in the other. For a while it seemed that she would carry it off, but then she tripped on her train, toppled the statue of the Virgin, and accidentally knocked Cavaradossi senseless with the horseshoe. Fortunately, as he was a tenor, the difference was not noticeable.

In the second act, the soprano couldn't pick up the knife without releasing her good luck tokens, so she was forced to dispatch the more insulted than injured Scarpia with a rodent extremity. At the climax of the opera, she ran behind the set, sang "O Scarpia, dietro a Dio," and jumped onto the parapet. As he watched her waving over her shoulder for the curtain call, Cazuti commented, "And I always thought tenors a little backward."

A Clockwork Spring

In an 1882 performance of *Siegfried*, the combination of an impetuous tenor and an inexperienced stage manager resulted in the title character's being eaten by the mechanical dragon. The audience was shocked but could do nothing: the Bayreuth tradition of absolute quiet during the performance prevented them from acting until the intermission, by which time the tenor was beyond help. Moreover, they realized that the music was really much nicer without all the shouting. Wagner agreed, and when he died the following year, it was rumored that he was designing a new dragon that could accommodate all the singers in the *Ring*.

A Bedraggled Grass Skirt

After *Lakmé*, the French were briefly infatuated with all things Southeast Asian. *La Fille de Manille, Les Burma Cheveux*, and *J'Avais Java* were typical extravaganzas with countless natives dancing before temples in exotic jungle settings. The fad was beginning to fade, but *La Coeur de Bali* revived the public's interest when a heavily tranquilized elephant brought in for the sacrifice scene suddenly got a case of the munchies and ate the costuming off the entire ladies' chorus. The scene proved so popular it was transplanted intact to the Folies Bergère and the elephant was awarded the Cordon Vert de l'Herbe.

A Bloody Dagger

While this might serve as a prop for almost any opera, it is in fact a grim reminder of the famous Dueling Giocondas. Through a clerical blunder, both Loretta Prevotsky and Barbara Winn-Dixie were hired to sing the same performance of *La Gioconda* at La Scala. With the usual backstage confusion, they did not discover the error until both entered tugging a more than usually bewildered La Cieca in opposite directions. Neither soprano wishing to leave the stage, the performance quickly developed into an astonishing duel of vocal technique and temperament, egged on by a wildly enthusiastic audience.

At the curtain calls for each of the first three acts, the admirers of each of the divas went mad for their own favorite, and it looked as if the evening would end in a draw. But before the last act, Prevotsky tricked her rival into a locked broom closet and prepared to revel in uncontested glory. She was about to launch into the "Suicidio" when she heard the sound of splintering wood and was confronted by her red-faced co-soprano.

Paraphrasing Boito, Winn-Dixie sang out, "Homicidio!" and plunged the dagger. In the subsequent trial, she pleaded not guilty by virtue of the so-called "Lucia" defense, which held that any performer on an opera stage was by definition insane. The judge, a true opera buff, sentenced her to ten years, ruling that she couldn't enter a *bel canto* plea for a *verismo* crime.

THE BEST OPERA EVER WRITTEN

Which is the best opera ever written? This question would seem to have as many answers as there are opera lovers, each choosing according to his preferences. But now at last science has given us an infallible means to know the truth once and for all:

$$\frac{\dfrac{T + A}{C} \times I}{H\,L}$$

This is the famous EIEIO (Einstein's Integer Equating Individual Operas), discovered in 1982 by Gary Einstein, a brilliant but erratic box office employee at a major New York opera company. Known also as the Theory of Sellativity, it has been used by opera house managements as a secret tool for determining the box office potential of projected productions. It is being made public here for the first time. Following are the definitions of the variables:

T = Number of Hit Tunes
Hit tunes are easily identified by listening for humming on the way out of the opera house. The one problem is presented by Wagner's leitmotifs, since a work like the *Ring* contains several catchy tunes, each no more than three seconds long. For purposes of the equation, a tune is defined as at least thirty seconds in length.

A = Activity Factor
Each opera is rated from 1 to 5 according to the amount of movement, such as dances, chorus milling, sword fights, jumping off parapets, i.e., anything that helps keep you awake.

C = Number of Major Characters
Major characters are those who sing high notes.

T + A Tunes plus Action
divided by
C Characters
tells us how much pleasure is afforded by each singer in the opera.

That pleasure is multiplied by:

I = Number of Intermissions
Nothing increases the pleasure of an opera more than the chance to stretch your legs, get a drink, and tell lies to other operagoers.

The result is in turn divided by:

H = Number of Hours
in the performance, rounded off to the nearest hour. For Wagner, round off to the nearest day.

multiplied by:

L = Language Factor
This number is based on how pleasant it is to listen to a particular language for several hours. For Italian or French, the factor is 1; for German, 2; for Russian or Slavic tongues, 3; for Sanskrit, Esperanto, or anything else, 4. Except for English, which rates

8, because there's nothing more irritating than not understanding your own language.

Let's do the math on some major operas and see who comes out the winner.

Le Nozze di Figaro: 9 Hit Tunes. Peasant dances, farcical doings, and jumping out of windows for a nice 3 Activity Factor. 3 Intermissions. Here's the weak point: 9 Major Characters. 4 Hours. Language Factor of 1. Final score: 1.

La Traviata: 8 Tunes. Not much Activity: 2. 2 Intermissions. 3 Major Characters. 3 Hours. Language Factor of 1. Final score: 2.22.

Cavalleria Rusticana

Die Walküre: 3 recognizable Tunes. One fight and some galloping about for a 2 Activity Factor. 2 Intermissions. 13 Major Characters (There's your problem, Richard). 5 Hours. Language Factor, 2. Final score, a pitiful .0769.

Pelléas et Mélisande: No Hit Tunes, Activity, or Characters with high notes. 4 Intermissions. 3 Hours. Final score: an inscrutable 0.

La Bohème: 10 Tunes. Mock fights, dances, Christmas Eve in the Latin Quarter for a big 5 on Activity. 3 Intermissions. 4 Major Characters. A trim 3 Hours. Language Factor of 1. Final score: 3.75.

Ladies and gentlemen, we have a winner!

La Bohème is the clear favorite. In fact, if we proposed a perfect single act of an opera, it would be Act II of **La Bohème**. A major Hit Tune ("Quando me'n vo' "), big ensembles, people milling about, a whole marching band, and exactly eighteen minutes from intermission to intermission. Now *that's* opera!

We should point out that some companies combine the first and second acts of **La Bohème**, giving it a score of only 2.5, and perform the four-act version of **La Traviata**, giving it a score of 3.33. This is blatant favoritism and chicanery, probably promoted and paid for by the house of Ricordi, Verdi's publishers. We regard the composer's original wishes as sacrosanct and stand by our findings.

SCHWANBRAINE

An Ignored Opera by Wagner

Schwanbraine is that rarest of all operas: a work by an established genius of which everyone is aware but which no one wants to see performed. Wagner chose the obscure German folk tale of the title and began composing the vocal music in 1849, shortly after the completion of *Lohengrin*. When his political and personal entanglements caused him to flee to Switzerland, he abandoned the manuscript.

In 1851 he published *Oper und Drama*, his artistic credo. This work espoused the use of leitmotifs, short musical phrases that evoke a particular idea or character and thus comment on or illustrate the onstage action. This technique would be brought to brilliant fruition in the *Ring, Die Meistersinger,* and *Tristan und Isolde*. First, though, there was *Schwanbraine*.

79

With all the vocal music composed in Wagner's previous, more romantic style, and all the orchestration in his most didactic leitmotif, the result suffers from an inner conflict, akin, some say, to attending an all-Berg orchestral concert while listening to Oldies but Goodies on headphones. Even King Ludwig of Bavaria could not bring himself to listen to this work more than once. In his famous castle, Neuschwanstein, where all the great rooms and halls were decorated with scenes from Wagner, Schwanbraine appears only in a minor mural in the Royal Privy.

To convey some sense of the total experience of the work, we list the major leitmotifs with their corresponding stage actions. Since Wagner never named his leitmotifs, we have relied on the best scholarly authorities for the names and subjects quoted.

ACTION

Dawn.
The three Weird Sisters are playing tennis in the Rhine Valley.
As they have only one eye amongst them, they spend their time feeling around for the ball and singing the story of the three races that live in the Valley: the Schwanlungen, who live on the heights, the Schweinlungen, who live in the swamps, and the evil dwarves, the Aqualungen, who live beneath the waters of the Rhine itself.

The story of each race is recalled, from before the creation of the world to the present, spiced with anecdotes and irrelevant information. Once they all lived together in harmony in a great castle, but when it went co-op and they had to serve on the planning committee together, the three races swore eternal enmity and moved out on each other. Today, the eldest son of the Schwanlungen has turned

LEITMOTIFS

DAWN
FATE FOREBODING
VALLEY VOLLEY
EYE'LL BE SEEING YOU
ALL THREE OLD FAMILIAR FACES
EYE ON THE BALL

VALLEY TALLY
GOOD
BAD

UGLY

DROWN IN THE VALLEY
VALLEY SOLO

BEGINNING
ORATIONS
REVELATIONS
EVERYMAN FOR HIMSELF
DUNGEON DUDGEON
OPERATE COOPERATE
MALICE IN THE PALACE

CASTLE HASSLE

OAF

Three
Weird Sisters

sixteen and taken the traditional blood vow of his race to kill a Schweinlung before the sun goes down. The whole clan is to gather on this spot in five minutes to renew the oath by spitting in the Rhine. As they haven't been invited to the party, the Weird Sisters hastily pack their tennis gear and set out to take the water at Bad Rubbish.

OATH
SECTS AND VIOLENCE
GROUP GRIPE

GREAT EXPECTORATIONS

RACKET
GOOD RIDDANCE

The next 42 minutes are taken up with the entrance of the clan of the Schwanlungen. They sing of what a nice day it is and of the greatness of German beer.

BOMBAST POMP CIRCUMSTANCE
PERSIFLAGE HOT AIR
EXTREME LOUDNESS
GUTEN TAG
TEUTON GROG

Schwanbraine enters, agitated. The nobles congratulate him on his birthday, praise the hearty German people, and ask why he is upset. He explains the opera has been on now for an hour and a quarter and nothing has happened. Also, he has just looked into a limpid pond and seen his own reflection for the first time.
He was naturally pleased by his own Teutonic beauty but was somewhat surprised to discover a sword stuck through his head. The nobles hail the genius of German metallurgy. The greatest of the nobles, the Skingraf of Urthingia, steps forward to explain the sword. Schwanbraine's father, Schwankopf, was a great warrior who was unfortunately absentminded. He never lost a battle, but often fought

SQUIRMIN' GERMAN

ROOTIN' TEUTON

VITA BREVIS
HOURS LONGER

REFLECTIONS ON A GOLDEN POND

GENTLEMAN PREFERS BLOND

YOU GO THROUGH MY HEAD
METTLE
IRONY

HERE COMES THE DRUDGE

the wrong country, leading all of middle Europe to declare war on the Schwanlungen as a means of keeping Schwankopf from attacking them. Wanting to give his son his fabled broadsword on his seventeenth birthday, he was afraid he would forget, so he put it through his three-year-old's brainpan, the most obvious spot that wouldn't be in anyone's way. He then forgot and fought several more battles with the sword before he was mortally wounded and the sword and its passenger consigned to the nursery. The sword has gone completely unnoticed by the Schwanlung heir, except for the occasional odd moment of wondering why no one else had to go through doors sideways.

As the Skingraf's narrative comes to an end, Schwanbraine awakens everyone by asking the sword's name. " 'Ausgang,' your father called it, because it gave him a quick way out of any trouble."

The nobles sing of the beauty of German consonants. Schwanbraine vows to kill a Schweinlungen with his new sword before the day is out. The Skingraf suggests it might be easier if he first took it out of his skull. Schwanbraine is not at all sure, but realizing that nothing has happened in the first two hours of the opera, he decides to give it a try. The nobles sing of the genius of German architecture and antiquarian

(During this deeply moving and intensely enervating recitation, the orchestra traditionally rehearses Mahler's Second Symphony for next week's subscription concert. They have time to do it twice.)

REVEILLE
GOURD SWORD
SWORD CHORD

EXIT WOUND

GLOTTALS TOP

USING HIS HEAD

IT STICKS IN HIS MIND

NOTHING DOING

NOTHING TO LOSE BUT HIS BRAINS

DEUTSCHE TREAT

$\longrightarrow$

REN

research. Schwanbraine tries to pull out the sword, but finds he can't get the hilt through his head. The Skingraf suggests he try pulling it from the other end, which is a great improvement. He wipes the sword off and waves it gleefully while the nobles revive their ladies and sing of previous German engagements they have just remembered.

GET THE POINT

HILT-IN-HEAD, NORSE CAROLINA

HAFT TO GO

DISCRETE NAUSEA

NO STRAIN, WIR GEHEN

Left alone, Schwanbraine is astonished to discover that the removal of the sword has left him able to think. Great thoughts flit through his brain, and he decides he will have to ponder them one of these days when he is less busy.

OPEN-MINDED

FLASH IN THE BRAIN PAN

MEDULLA OBBLIGATO

He hides behind the bushes to await the first Schweinlungen to

OPENING IN THE REEDS

happen along. As luck would have
it, it is a woman, coming to take   LADY'S FIRST
a bath, a habit of which
Schwanbraine has never heard. As he   DIRTY MIND
watches rapturously, she removes
her outer garments. Then she   HEALTHY BODY
slips out of her tunic and jerkin
as his eyes grow wider. Finally,   PRINCIPAL'S GROWING INTEREST
as the sweat breaks out on his
brow, she takes off her brMODESTY VIRGINITY MAIDENHOOD
and slips beneath the water. In   LADY GO DIVER
a fury, Schwanbraine leaps into   LADY IN THE LAKE
the orchestra pit and slaughters
the bassoonist who played the
MODESTY leitmotif. Climbing back   OPENING IN THE REEDS
onto the stage, he finds the maiden
hastily toweling off and tries   EINS ZWEI DRY
to introduce himself to her.

The Schweinlung maiden, named
Schweinknoechel, is immediately   HELLO
smitten by the way the light plays
on his blond hair, glints off his   HALO
white teeth, and shines through his
head. She sings a lengthy ode to   HOLLOW
the sun. He responds rapturously   SOLAR ELEGY
about a crisp winter's day. She   JOY HAPPINESS
enthuses about jumping into big   YOUTH SPRING LOVE
piles of leaves. He sings   ENERGY FUN PUBERTY
joyously of biting off   SAP RISING NEW GROWTH ADVENTURE
young saplings in the   SWEET SIXTEEN FIRST DATE HOPE
spring. They are   COURAGE STRENGTH VITALITY EXUBERANCE
about to launch   HERO LIGHT RICHARD'S WHISKERS GREEN
into a duet   GROWTH ECSTASY MADE HER RAVE FRIVOLITY
when they   RADIANCE BEAUTY MINNA BOUGHT HIM SPRING
realize   INTOXICATION LIFE BURMA SHAVE INFATUATION
the le-   WILLOW IN A WINDSTORM KITTEN ON A STRING MELANCHOLY
itmo-   YOUNGER SPRINGTIME ANGEL AND LOVER, HEAVEN AND EARTH
tifs SUPERCALIFRAGILISTICEXPIALIDOCIOUS VERNAL EQUINOX
have   MILD EUPHORIA PICTURE YOUR LEITMOTIF HERE FILLER
run   GAMBOLING EXTREME PLEASURE MODIFIED RAPTURE TIME

→

```
a   GERMAN ART  F U CN RD THIS  CONTRACT NEGOTIATIONS
m   SCHNITZEL U MA HV A CRER HOURLY WAGE  SWEAT SHOP
o   FRANKFURTERS  IN OFC SVCS  FRINGE BENEFITS  LOCAL 802
k   HAMBURGERS  FR FRTR INFO CALL  STRIKE  STRIKE  STRIKE
.
```

Just in the nick of time, the musicians' union demands a lunch break, since the orchestra has now been playing nonstop for four hours. Schwanbraine seizes the opportunity to sing all the leitmotifs himself. His newly unencumbered head is brimming with ideas. Why should the Schwanlungen and the Schweinlungen be enemies? Why can't all men live in peace and harmony? Why can't women be the equals of men? Schweinknoechel asks if this is a riddle. He then notices that she has a pair of knitting needles stuck through her head. When he suggests she remove them and join him in thinking great thoughts, she laughs and says he's crazy but she loves him. In an unfortunate choice of words, he says he can't believe it. ''No?'' she says, ''then I will prove it.'' She then jumps into the river and drowns. The chorus of nobles returns to sing of the steadfastness and simplemindedness of German womenfolk. Schwanbraine decides he has had enough of great thoughts and wistfully reinserts the sword into his head as the chorus lauds German cuisine and sings that they'd like to get something to eat in the wurst way.

CURTAIN

(About ten minutes later, the orchestra comes back from its break and plays the Leonore Overture no. 4.)

IF THEY COULD ONLY SING

Some Special Casts We Would Like to See

Opera is becoming more and more visible on television and in the movies. Yet, if opera is to be fully accepted in these media, it will have to use established stars in leading roles. Imagine the thrill of seeing Robert Redford as Alfredo with Meryl Streep as Violetta. Or Sylvester Stallone as Manrico, the original Italian Stallion.

Or Gary Coleman as Amahl. Or Joanne Woodward outdoing her own *Three Faces of Eve* as the four heroines of *Tales of Hoffmann*. With good lip-synching and Marni Nixon to fill in the voices, any major star can also be an opera star. Here are a few ideal movie and TV opera casts drawn with a sharp eye on box office and Nielsen ratings.

The Barber of Seville

Fiorello:	Zeppo
Almaviva:	Allan Jones
Figaro:	Harpo
Rosina:	Kitty Carlisle
Dr. Bartolo:	Groucho
Don Basilio:	Chico
Bertha:	Margaret Dumont

Turandot

Turandot:	Dolores Del Rio
Liù:	Olivia de Havilland
Calaf:	Errol Flynn
Timur:	Lewis Stone
Ping:	Moe
Pang:	Larry
Pong:	Curly
The Emperor:	Sam Jaffe

La Bohème

Marcello:	Morey Amsterdam
Rodolfo:	Dick van Dyke
Colline:	Richard Deacon
Schaunard:	Jerry Paris
Benoit/Alcindoro:	Carl Reiner
Mimi:	Mary Tyler Moore
Musetta:	Rose Marie

Così Fan Tutte

Fiordiligi:	Lucille Ball
Dorabella:	Vivian Vance
Despina:	Joan Davis
Ferrando:	Desi Arnaz
Guglielmo:	William Frawley
Don Alfonso:	Jim Backus

Der Rosenkavalier

Octavian:	Dustin Hoffman
The Marschallin:	Teri Garr
Baron Ochs:	Charles Durning
Sophie:	Jessica Lange
Faninal:	Sydney Pollack
Valzacchi:	Dabney Coleman
The Italian Singer:	Bill Murray

The Magic Flute

Tamino:	Mickey
Three Ladies:	Cinderella's Stepmother and Stepsisters
Papageno:	Goofy
The Queen of the Night:	Cruella deVil
Monostatos:	Donald Duck
Pamina:	Minnie

→

Three Genii:	Huey, Dewey, Louie	**Das Rheingold**	
Sarastro:	Doc	Woglinde:	Victoria Principal
The Speaker:	Grumpy	Wellgunde:	Priscilla Presley
First Priest:	Sleepy	Flosshilde:	Linda Gray
Second Priest:	Sneezy	Alberich:	Larry Hagman
Two Men in Armor:	Happy, Dopey	Fricka:	Linda Evans
Papagena:	Bashful (in drag)	Wotan:	John Forsythe
		Freia:	Diahann Carroll
Elektra		Fasolt:	Jim Davis
		Fafner:	Howard Keel
Elektra:	Gypsy Rose Lee	Froh:	Helmut Berger
Chrysothemis:	June Havoc	Donner:	Rock Hudson
Klytemnestra:	Joan Crawford	Loge:	George Hamilton
		Mime:	Patrick Duffy
		Erda:	Joan Collins

Lady Godiva

90

AFTER THE OPERA

You've slept through the performance and you run into some friends who want to discuss it. You now face your truest test as an operagoer. All your hard work may go for nothing if you blow your curtain calls, so to speak.

Here is the most important rule of any post-performance analysis: Always complain about something. Among opera fans, praising a performance puts you out on a limb; knocking it is always safe. If it was a bad performance, everyone will agree; if it

was a good performance, everyone will still admit there is something in what you say; if it was a great performance, everybody will be envious that your standards are so much higher than theirs.

Here are a few guidelines to what you can safely say about any performance:

1. The Soprano: Her voice has lost that luster. The vibrato is getting wider. It's just not the same since she had that vocal problem. (Almost every singer has had a vocal problem.)

2. The Tenor: His singing was all right, but oh! that acting. (This works for all tenors but Jon Vickers. For him, you love the acting, but you're not crazy about his vocal mannerisms.) The big aria was transposed down a half-step.

3. The Baritone or Bass: He's pushing. The basic sound is good, but he covers on top. He seemed to be marking until the big aria. (It helps if you know the name of the big aria, but if not, everyone will still know the one you mean.)

4. The Mezzo or Contralto: She's developing a hoot. Perhaps she's really a soprano.

5. The Conductor: He drowned out the singers. He couldn't keep the ensemble together. He couldn't follow the singers. He let the singers walk all over him. He's just using this as rehearsal time for when he conducts it at Bayreuth next summer.

6. The Production: Too traditional for your tastes. Why do a new production if you don't have new insights? (Unless Jean-Pierre Ponnelle is the director. Then decry the lack of respect for the composer's inten-

tions and change for the sake of change.)

If all else fails, mention Callas. For your money, no one else has ever measured up to her performance of the role. (It doesn't matter what role, she sang them all.) Don't talk about her voice, but you can't forget how she used her hands. If pressed, say it was indescribable. The true opera fan will nod reverently and switch the topic to his pirate records.

ABOUT THE AUTHOR

William J. Brooke lives in New York City with two newts and a mezzo. He is married to the mezzo but admits only to the most platonic relationship with the newts.

He is a sometime singer of opera and operetta who works full-time in an unsung capacity at a major metropolitan opera house. He has previously published a book about Christmas, and his books for musical revues have been performed Off-Broadway and out of the country, in that order.

Published by Spectacle Lane Press